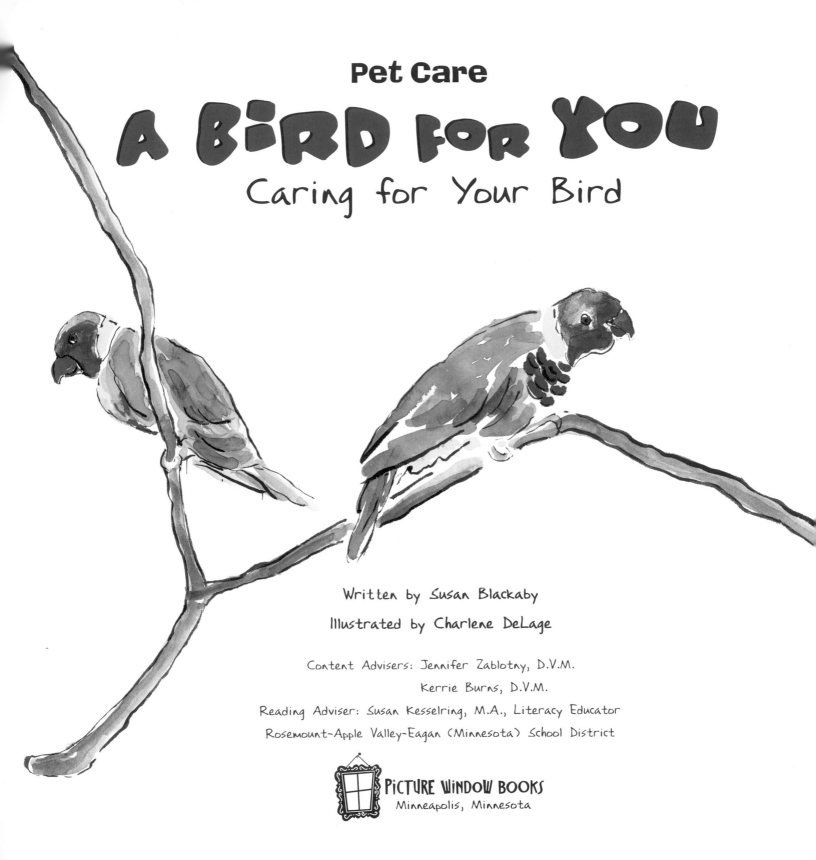

Pet Care

A BiRD FOR YOU

Caring for Your Bird

Written by Susan Blackaby

Illustrated by Charlene DeLage

Content Advisers: Jennifer Zablotny, D.V.M.

Kerrie Burns, D.V.M.

Reading Adviser: Susan Kesselring, M.A., Literacy Educator

Rosemount-Apple Valley-Eagan (Minnesota) School District

PiCTURE WiNDOW BOOKS

Minneapolis, Minnesota

Editor: Nadia Higgins
Designer: Nathan Gassman
Page production: Picture Window Books
The illustrations in this book were painted with watercolor.

Picture Window Books
5115 Excelsior Boulevard
Suite 232
Minneapolis, MN 55416
1-877-845-8392
www.picturewindowbooks.com

Printed in the United States of America.
1 2 3 4 5 6 08 07 06 05 04 03

Library of Congress Cataloging-in-Publication Data
Blackaby, Susan.
A bird for you : caring for your bird / written by Susan Blackaby ; illustrated by Charlene DeLage.
v. cm. — (Pet care)
Contents: A bird for a pet—Choosing a cage—A place for a cage—Cage care—Food for birds—Bird games—Make
your own bird book—Fun facts—How birds behave.
ISBN 1-4048-0117-0 (lib. bdg.)
1. Cage birds—Juvenile literature. [1. Birds as pets.] 1. DeLage, Charlene, 1944- ill. II. Title.
SF461.35 .B58 2003
636.6'8—dc21
2002154997

TABLE OF CONTENTS

A Bird for a Pet

Do you like to watch wild birds?

Then you might like to have a bird for a pet.

There are all kinds of tame birds that make good pets.
Some birds sing. Some birds talk. Some birds do tricks.

These are some small songbirds.

They do not like to be held but are fun to watch.

dove

finch

canary

These birds are in the parrot family.

They love to cuddle and show off.

Some of them are noisy chatterboxes.

lovebirds

conure

cockatiel

7

Choosing a Cage

All birds need enough space to flap their wings.

Some fly or hop from perch to perch.

Get a wide cage to give your bird room to move.

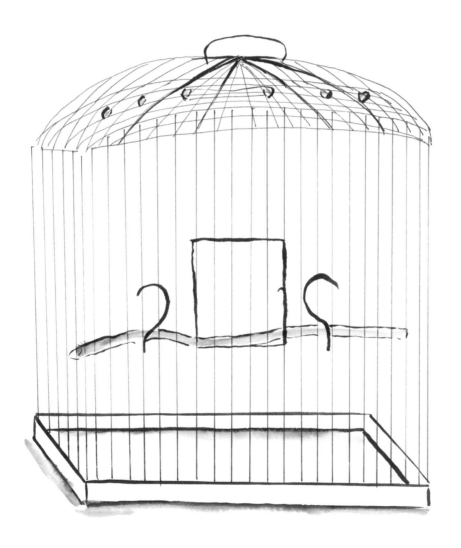

Long-tailed birds need room to stretch out.

Some parrots and parakeets like to climb.

Get a wide, tall cage with strong bars.

Perches are good for your bird's toes and feet.
Get more than one perch in more than one shape.
Choose perches that feel different from each other.
Set the perches away from the food and water.

Each bird needs 3 inches ($7\frac{1}{2}$ centimeters) of perch space.

Little birds can use small plastic feeders and water bottles.
Bigger birds need sturdy dishes that won't tip over.

A Place for a Cage

Set the cage in a safe place.
Give your bird lots of light.
Be sure the space is not
too hot or too drafty.

Birds can be fraidy cats!

Loud noises scare them.

Keep your bird's cage in a quiet place.

- Do not put the cage in the kitchen.
- Do not put the cage close to a TV.
- Do not put the cage near a heater.

Cage Care

Cover the bottom of the birdcage with bedding.

Use wood shavings or black-and-white newspaper.

Change the bedding every two days.
Clean the whole cage every two weeks.

Food for Birds

Feed your bird the special seeds
or pellets made for each breed.
Your bird also needs plenty of
chopped fruits and vegetables.
Give your bird a cuttlebone
or mineral block to peck.
This sharpens and trims its beak.

Birds can be very messy eaters!
Keep hulls and shells out of the dishes in the cage.
Do not let fresh food spoil in the cage.

Feeding Tips

Good to Eat
- Peppers
- Broccoli
- Sweet potatoes
- Peas
- Cantaloupe
- Kiwi
- Chopped hard-cooked eggs, including the shells

Bad to Eat
- Iceberg lettuce
- Cabbage
- Chocolate
- Coffee beans
- Avocado
- Dairy products

Give your bird clean, fresh water every day.

Wash your bird's feeders with soapy water every day.

Bird Games

Your bird can get bored!

Birds like to play in water.

A birdbath or a spray bottle will also help keep your bird clean.

Bells, rattles, and blocks make good toys.

Let your bird get out of the cage for some exercise every day.

Birds can be amazing pets.

Give your bird special care and love.

Your bird will be your best buddy.

Make Your Own Bird Book

Draw pictures to go with these bird sayings.

The first kid at the bus stop is an early bird.

This rainy weather is for the birds.

I feel as free as a bird.

My best pal and I are birds of a feather.

My silly brother acts like a birdbrain.

Fun Facts

- There are almost 8,500 species of birds.
- Some birds sing songs with as many as 80 notes per second.
- A macaw can live for 40 to 90 years.
- The bee hummingbird is the smallest bird in the world. It is about the same size as a bumblebee.
- Birds can't taste spicy foods. In fact, it's good to feed birds spicy hot peppers, because the peppers have lots of vitamin A.

Words to Know

bedding—soft material for lining the bottom of a pet's cage

breed—a kind of bird

cuttlebone—the rough, oval-shaped bone of a cuttlefish

pellets—small, dry pieces of food especially for pets

perch—a place for a bird to stand on, often made of a piece of rope or a wooden rod

mineral block—a hard, round board that gives a bird something to peck. A mineral block helps keep a bird's beak from growing too long.

How Birds Behave

Different kinds of birds act in different ways. This chart tells you about some of them.

	Clever	Friendly	Noisy	Good Singer	Can Talk
African grey parrot					✓
canary				✓	
cockatiel		✓			
cockatoo		✓			
conure	✓		✓		✓
dove				✓	
finch				✓	
lory	✓	✓			
lovebird		✓			
macaw	✓	✓			
parakeet		✓			✓

To Learn More

At the Library

Ada, Alma Flor. *Daniel's Pet.* San Diego: Harcourt, 2002.

Davis, Patricia Anne. *Brian's Bird.* Morton Grove, Ill.: A. Whitman, 2000.

Evans, Mark. *Birds.* (ASPCA Pet Care Guides for Kids). New York: Dorling Kindersley, 2001.

Frost, Helen. *Birds.* Mankato, Minn.: Pebble Books, 2001.

On the Web

ASPCA Kids' Site

http://www.animaland.org

For stories, games, and information about pets

Pet Station

http://www.petstation.com

For information on caring for birds and other animals

Want to learn more about birds?

Visit FACT HOUND at *http://www.facthound.com*.

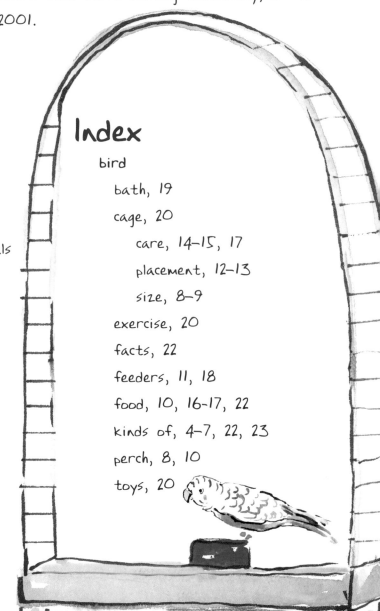